Alan Titchmarsh's Gardening Guides

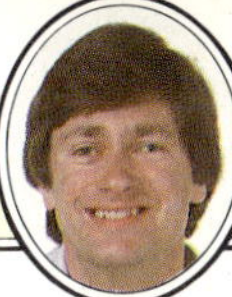

BUSH ROSES

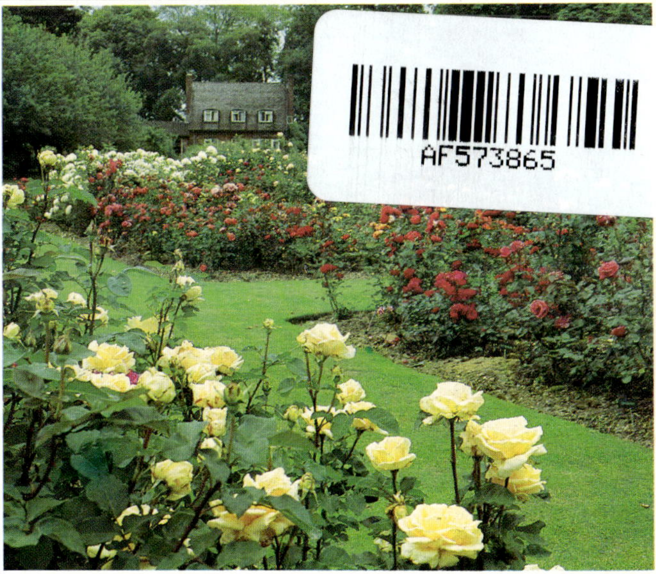

HAMLYN

London · New York · Sydney · Toronto

Coming up roses

'He who would have beautiful Roses in his garden must have beautiful Roses *in his heart'*, said the Dean of Rochester in 1869. It's a love affair that still flourishes. Today in country estates, suburban plots, bleak backyards and earth-filled pots you'll find roses doing their best to please, and usually succeeding.

Their willingness to survive is as much responsible for their popularity as their heady scents and ravishing colours, for few folk will bother growing a plant that is temperamental, however spectacular the flowers may be.

Thanks to years of shrewd observation and careful hybridisation by rose breeders, today's gardener can choose from an unrivalled collection of bush roses that possess the romantic attributes of scent and colour, plus the practical advantages of resistance to disease, a stocky habit, rain-tolerant blooms and a longer season of flowering. In short, the rose grower never had it so good.

This book concentrates on the modern roses of bushy habit (the ones that gardeners call hybrid teas and floribundas) and on the miniature varieties that are becoming deservedly popular. Thanks to these pocket-sized treasures, even if your garden is no more than a windowsill, you can still have roses all the way.

Which type?

Don't rush out to the garden centre or the shop until you've decided which kind of bush you want. Where do you want to grow it? What do you want it to do? Which shape of flower most appeals to you? Here's what each of the three main types has to offer:

Hybrid teas These are the fully double roses with plump and pointed centres that look like miniature cabbages. A new system of rose classification rules that we should now call them 'large-flowered roses', but it will be donkey's years before the old name bites the dust. Hybrid teas produce their large flowers singly, or with just a few side buds, atop strong stems. They usually pause for breath between their flushes of bloom but produce individual flowers that are prized in specimen vases and at flower shows. Choose your varieties carefully. Some of them are bred strictly for the exhibitor and their mammoth blooms may not stand up to wet weather.

Floribundas These are the very best bedding roses, for they carry their blooms in large sprays over a longer season than the hybrid teas. We're now supposed to call them 'cluster-flowered roses', which shows that each stem is capable of holding plenty of blooms. The flowers are usually open centred, but occasionally they resemble those of the hybrid tea, in shape if not in size, and they usually shrug off the rain better than their more portly relations. Generally they are not so fragrant as the hybrid teas, but powerfully scented new varieties are appearing and will eventually make such generalisations untrue.

Both hybrid teas and floribundas are available as standard roses. These are the 'lollipop' rose trees which are produced by grafting the chosen variety on to a tall stalk of wild rose or briar. Use them to add a bit of height to beds and borders, or where you need a floral full-stop.

Miniatures Gardeners who groan that they haven't room for roses can escape no longer. The miniatures have leapt into the limelight and show no signs of stepping aside. Their flowers are small, but then so are they, which

Above: Bush roses planted in blocks of one colour look most effective. *Opposite:* Miniature rose Baby Masquerade

means that they can be squeezed into window boxes, pots and tubs to decorate doorsteps and ledges. Many miniatures are under 30 cm (1 ft) high, but be prepared for some of them to grow up to 45 cm (18 in). As flower-bed edgers they more than earn their keep from late spring until autumn, especially if kept well fed and watered (their

roots are nearer the surface than those of their larger relations). A little winter pruning and treatment against pests and diseases will act as a further guarantee that they remain in the pink.

Miniatures are often sold as house plants and, if you've time to pander to their whims, they can survive indoors all the year round. The trouble is, they need cool temperatures, brilliant light and reasonable humidity to do well. Failing that, they'll be spindly and crawling with bugs after only a few weeks. The best solution for the busy gardener is to keep the miniatures indoors during their first flush of bloom, and then to plant them out in the garden for the rest of their lives. They'll be happy then.

How to use roses

You don't have to grow roses in beds by themselves, even though they do look spectacular when massed. Try using them to give height to beds and borders of herbaceous perennials, to bring colour to the front of shrubberies, and even as hedges. Any single row of roses planted close enough can be called a hedge, but some varieties (the hefty Queen Elizabeth for instance) particularly lend themselves to forming a flowering thicket. In most cases the bushes can be planted 60 cm (2 ft) apart, and you'll have to prune your hybrid tea or floribunda hedge just as you would the bushes on their own if you want to make sure that disease stays away and the flowers stay within view, especially on Queen Elizabeth.

If you do decide to plant your roses in beds, the effect will be ten times more stunning if the bushes are all of the same variety. A patchwork quilt effect (with one of each of a dozen varieties) will be pretty but not half so head-turning as a one-colour bonanza.

In the never-ending war against weeds, don't forget that some roses make dainty ground cover. You'll have to weed between them in the early months of establishment (you'll need thorn-proof gloves) but once they've thickened up, the weeds will have a job to push through. Few of the hybrid teas and floribundas are of use here, but miniatures like Snow Carpet are. And like other miniatures, this variety is happy in containers, too.

Buying roses

The first rose bushes I ever had came from a High Street store and were wrapped in polythene bags complete with pretty picture. Not a leaf was to be seen and the stems were covered in wax. In they went and up they came, to grow into some of the best bushes I've ever had. Some folk sneer at pre-packed roses. Not I. Even if they convince me that such bushes are not first grade, I reckon that with a good start in decent soil you'd be hard pushed to tell the difference between one of these and a posh container-grown plant from thc gardcn ccntrc a ycar aftcr planting. Their only disadvantage is that the choice of varieties is limited. Mind you, do make sure you buy them fresh, while the buds are still tight. Any that have produced long, pale shoots have been in the shop too long and won't take kindly to the cold outside.

Roses purchased by mail order from specialist nurseries are invariably good value for money. You can take your time choosing from fat descriptive catalogues and often find rare beauties that are unobtainable elsewhere. Order in summer, if you can (once you've seen the rose you want in someone else's garden) and the grower will send you your plant in autumn.

Beware of ordering from 'Special Offer' adverts in newspapers where the advertiser makes stupendous and exaggerated claims for his plants. Usually they'll be small and something less than exciting when they arrive.

Both mail-order roses and those that are pre-packed will be sold 'bare-root' – that is, no soil will be clinging to the roots. This is no problem in the dormant season, between November and March, provided the roots are

Floribunda rose Queen Elizabeth grown as a hedge

A perfect bloom – Pink Favourite a popular hybrid tea

not allowed to dry out. Soak them overnight in a bucket of water before you plant. If they arrive through the post when the weather's foul, they'll sit happily in their wrapping for a few days, provided they're kept cool. Then unpack them, remove any straw or polythene from their roots and (if you still can't plant them properly in their final resting place) bury them in a hole dug in the garden, leaving the stems sticking out. They'll be happy like this for several weeks.

Nurseries and garden centres sell roses in large pots.

Soak bare-rooted plants in water overnight before planting

They're known in the trade as container-grown stock and their advantage is that they can be planted at any time of year – not just in the dormant season as with bare-root roses. It's essential that the plants have been well established in their pots so that any check at planting time is minimised, and the great advantage from your point of view is that, during the summer, you can see the exact colouring and sample the perfume of the open flowers. Disadvantages? Expense is the only one. You'll pay a little more for a pot-grown plant.

Miniatures are nearly always sold in pots and it's a

good thing. They have smaller, more fibrous root systems than the larger bush roses and would dry out much more quickly if sold bare-root.

What to look for

If you're buying through mail order you'll have to trust the nurseryman. If you're buying from a nursery or garden centre, look for healthy plants with at least three strong stems. Avoid bushes that have diseased foliage. Bare-root bushes from High Street stores should have the regulation three stems plus a good root system that's preferably not one sided. Sometimes there's no way of seeing the roots and you'll have to take a risk. But then these roses are the cheapest of all.

Where to plant

Bush roses love sun; it's mother's milk to them and if you deprive them of it you'll get fewer flowers. Find them a spot that's bright and they'll seldom disappoint you.

You'll read a lot about how roses need clay soil to thrive. It's rot. Roses are thirsty and don't perform well when deprived of water, but if your garden is full of dry, sandy soil that doesn't mean you can't grow them. It does mean that you'll have to dig in plenty of moisture-holding organic matter and that it will be a good idea to keep a sprinkler handy in summer, but if you do that you'll produce excellent roses.

Avoid replanting roses on ground that has supported them for generations. Soil can become 'sick' of roses. Not in the accepted sense of the word, but the plants refuse to flourish on ground that their ancestors have milked dry. Move them to a fresh site.

Planting

Whatever the soil it's a good idea to dig it over before planting. Single digging (to the depth of one spade blade) will usually be adequate, but enthusiasts who believe that the nastier the medicine the more good it does you will want to double dig. This involves digging to the depth of two spade blades and it's hell on the back! Me? I'll settle for single digging and for working in plenty of organic matter – well-rotted manure or compost, peat, leafmould, spent mushroom compost or whatever I can lay my spade on. With roses, what goes in must come up.

Dig over the ground a good month before you plant so that it can settle in the meantime. Then, about a week before planting, scatter a handful of blood, bone and fishmeal over each square metre (yard) of earth. It does more good than the oft-recommended bonemeal alone.

As far as soil acidity goes, roses prefer a soil that's on the acid side – around pH 6.5. If your ground is chalky, bung in plenty of organic enrichment and the bushes should survive, unless the soil is on top of layers of chalk and so shallow that they just can't extract any sustenance.

One final word on moisture: although the bushes are said to love clay, they won't tolerate bad drainage. If your ground is forever standing in water, drain it, or change from growing roses to bulrushes.

Planting in containers

If your roses have to be in pots, tubs and boxes, make sure the containers are large enough to allow for a bit of root growth. Pots 23 cm (9 in) in diameter will suit the miniatures, which can be moved up to 30-cm (12-in) pots when they need more space. The larger bush roses will be happiest in tubs if they have to be confined. As to compost, use that sold as John Innes No.3 potting compost. It's weighty enough to hold the containers firm and it offers plenty of nourishment. What's more, it won't shrink from the sides of the container as peaty compost does when it gets dry.

A layer of broken flowerpots or pebbles over the base of the container will make sure that drainage is good, provided that plenty of holes are present to allow surplus water to escape.

When to plant

- Bare-root plants: between November and March
- Container-grown plants: any time of year. But never plant when the ground is dust dry, wet and muddy or frozen solid.

How to plant

With your ground prepared and your bushes waiting you're ready to plant. Here's what to do:

Bare-root plants

1. Soak the roots well in a bucket of water.
2. Snip off any broken or damaged roots, and shorten any long ones to around 23 cm (9 in).
3. Dig a hole large enough to accommodate all the roots when spread out.
4. Sit the plant in the hole so that the old soil mark on the stem is just below the new soil surface. The point at which the green stems meet the fat rootstock should rest about 2.5 cm (1 in) below soil level.
5. Replace the soil, firming it with your foot as you do so.

When the job is finished, level the soil around the plant with a fork to make a neat finish.

6. If the soil is at all dry (unlikely in winter) give it a good soak – 9 litres (a couple of gallons) will do nicely.

Container-grown plants

1. Water the container well.
2. Dig a hole large enough to take the rootball.
3. Remove the pot or plastic container but don't disturb the roots.
4. Plant so that the surface of the compost in the pot rests just below the new soil level.
5. Replace and re-firm the soil.
6. Water the plant in.

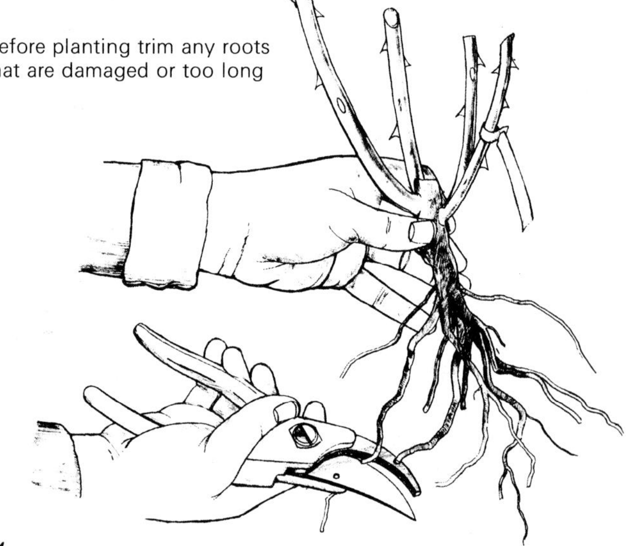

Before planting trim any roots that are damaged or too long

(a) Position bush at correct depth and spread out roots
(b) Replace soil, firming as you go. Ensure graft point is below soil level

(a) Slit container, keeping rootball intact
(b) Position rootball at correct depth

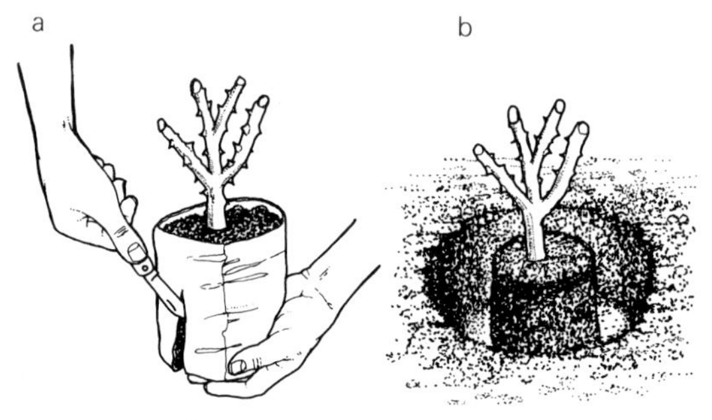

Floribunda rose Anne Harkness (see page 27)

Spacing

Both hybrid teas and floribundas growing in beds should be spaced 60 cm (2 ft) apart to allow them room to grow. Miniatures can be spaced 30 cm (1 ft) apart.

Planting standards

Standards should be prepared and planted exactly like bush roses but they will need staking. Knock the stake into the ground once the hole has been dug but before the plant is put in. The top of the stake should rest just below the head of branches when planting is completed, and two proprietary plant ties should fasten stem to stake at the top and about one third of the way up.

If you're planting a row of standards, space them out at least 2 m (6 ft) apart.

Hybrid tea rose National Trust (see page 26)

Caring for your roses

Once they are established, there are a few regular jobs that need to be done to keep your roses in good shape.

Pruning

It strikes terror into most people's hearts, but there's no doubt about it – pruning is vital. It keeps your bushes shapely, within bounds, and producing plenty of blooms. What's more it helps to keep down disfiguring diseases, so take your courage in both hands and a pair of secateurs in one of them.

New roses Roses planted between November and March should be attacked fiercely, and this really does take nerve. Cut all the stems on a new hybrid tea back to within 8 or 10 cm (3 or 4 in) of the ground, making your cuts just above outward-facing buds. The buds will be no more than little red dots in some cases, so you'll have to look hard. New floribundas should be similarly pruned, but cut these back to around 15 cm (6 in).

It is important to make a correct cut when pruning: (a) is cut too close to the bud; (b) too far from the bud; (c) angle of cut is wrong; (d) correctly cut

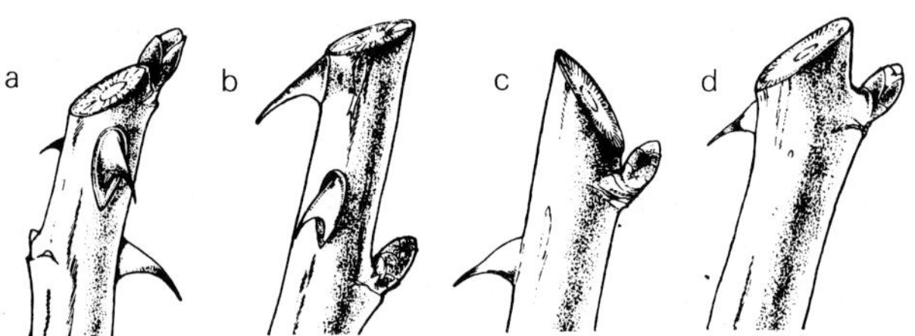

This drastic pruning makes sure that in the first year the bushes produce a strong framework of branches. You'll still get some flowers in the first season, so don't worry.

Miniatures don't need hard pruning after planting but can be pruned each year as described below.

New standard roses planted between November and March should be pruned back to within 10 cm (4 in) of the top of the main stem, if they are hybrid teas, and to within 15 cm (6 in) of it if they are floribundas. Any subsequent pruning is as for hybrid teas and floribundas, except that your bush will be sitting on a tall stalk.

Hybrid teas Mature hybrid teas (those that have been planted a year or more) are pruned at any time between January and mid-March. You'll need a sharp pair of secateurs, and if your bushes are old and gnarled you might need a pair of loppers and a pruning saw, too. This is what to do:

1. Take a long, hard look at your bush.
2. Cut out completely (right to the very bottom) any dead stems – they'll be dark brown, dry and brittle.
3. Cut out any weak and spindly stems and any that are growing inwards across the centre of the bush.
4. Cut out any stems that are damaged or diseased.
5. Hopefully you'll still have some stems left and, with any luck, they'll be arranged in a sort of goblet shape with an open centre. Six or eight stems at most are all you should retain.
6. Shorten all your remaining stems to just below knee height, cutting them off cleanly just above an outward-facing bud. This will help to keep the bush open centred and shapely when it starts to grow.

Pruning a bush rose:
(a) First remove any dead material, spindly growth or badly crossing stems.
(b) Shorten remaining stems to just below knee height.
(c) Pruning complete; note stems have all been cut back to an outward pointing bud

If your plants are neglected and overgrown, saw out a few of the really gnarled branches every winter for three years and the plants should soon become rejuvenated.

Floribundas Prune these in exactly the same way as hybrid teas, but when you've cut out all unwanted stems, shorten the rest to just *above* knee height. (I know some people have longer legs than others, but roses really aren't that fussy!)

Miniatures Instead of cutting the shoots back hard, thin them out a little to avoid overcrowding, and snip off any diseased stem tips. As with other bush roses, prune between January and March.

Summer pruning

Most bush roses will perform better if their dead flowerheads are removed. It saves them from wasting their energy on producing unwanted seeds, and it often

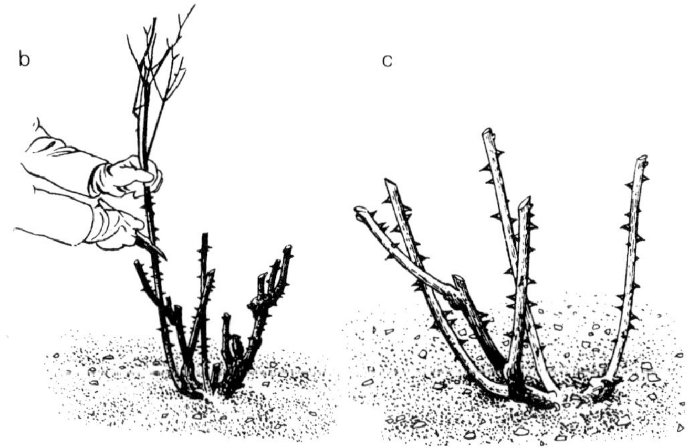

encourages a second flush of flowering.

As soon as the blooms fade on a particular stem, cut it back. Don't just snip off the top 8 or 10 cm (3 or 4 in), but remove about 30 cm (1 ft) of growth, cutting back into stem that is at least pencil thickness. Then the stems that re-grow will also be thick and can produce plenty of bloom. It's a tip that was passed on to me by an old gardener and it works a treat.

Watering

Roses in containers will depend on you for almost every drop of water they get, so don't be mean. Soak them thoroughly whenever the compost in the pot or tub looks slightly dry on the surface.

Roses planted in the garden should never be allowed to get thirsty during their first year of establishment. Turn a garden sprinkler on them for about two hours in dry spells, or give each bush about 9 litres (a couple of gallons) of water from a can. Once established the bushes will send their roots down deeply and seldom need any irrigation. But keep an eye on your miniatures – their roots are nearer the surface.

If you have to water hybrid teas in dry spells, or any rose whose blooms will not stand up to heavy drenching, avoid using the garden sprinkler. Instead, jam a watering-can rose on the end of a hosepipe and support this in the handle of a garden fork stuck into the soil. The water can be diverted on to the soil and away from the fragile flowers.

Feeding

Roses are greedy blighters, but feed them well and they'll give you a plentiful show of flowers. Mine get two feeds a year:

- Two handfuls of blood, bone and fishmeal scattered around each plant in April
- One handful of Tonks formula rose fertiliser scattered around each bush in June

The Tonks mixture contains magnesium and potash which really helps in promoting healthy growth and free flowering. Both applications can be lightly forked into the surface of the soil.

Suckers

Most rose bushes are propagated in the nursery by budding. This means that buds from the required variety are grafted on to the root system of a wild rose or briar. It's a technique that's useful to the nurseryman because his bushes can be grown to a saleable size very quickly, but it can be a pain in the neck for the gardener when the rootstock sends up its own shoots which will have different leaves and flowers to those of the chosen plant.

As soon as you see a sucker, get rid of it, otherwise it will quickly bring up its friends to swamp your bush. You'll probably recognise it by its rather ferny foliage, a paler green colouring, and sometimes (but not always) a larger number of leaflets. Scrape away the soil around the base of the bush and pull off the sucker at its point of origin. If you cut it off at soil level it will simply send up more shoots.

Mulching

If you can afford the time and money, lay a mulch around your bushes. This is an 8-cm (3-in) thick blanket of organic matter – peat, leafmould, manure or pulverised bark – that will keep in moisture and keep down weeds. Manure will also provide nutrients, but it may contain weed seeds, so be ready to knock the youngsters on the head with a hoe as soon as they emerge.

Weed control

You'll get weeds in your rose bed just as often as you find them anywhere else. Mulching is the best way to suppress them, but otherwise use a Dutch hoe – carefully. Dig too deeply with it and you'll damage the rose roots, and the damage may well encourage sucker growth.

Several rose-bed weedkillers are on the market and can be watered on to clean soil to keep down weeds for almost a year. However, if you use these preparations regularly, there's a danger that the bases of the rose stems may be permanently damaged. The stuff will stop you from growing other plants underneath your roses, too, which is a shame. I'd stick to the hoe and the mulch if I were you.

Making more roses

The professionals might propagate their roses by budding, but it's a fiddly hit and miss affair for unskilled hands. It's much easier for the average gardener to take hardwood cuttings.

Go over your bushes in late summer and autumn, snipping off pencil-thick stems. Use your secateurs to turn these stems into 23-cm (9-in) long cuttings, sliced neatly above a bud at the top and below a bud at the base.

Push a spade into a patch of spare ground to make a slit trench, and trickle some sand into the base. Push in each cutting so that just the top 8 cm (3 in) remains above soil level, then firm back the earth with your feet.

In one year's time these twigs will have turned into small bushes and they can then be dug up and moved to their chosen spots. They'll make smashing plants in a year or two, and you'll never have any problems with troublesome suckers!

Choosing your plants

Colour catalogues are packed with mouth-watering pictures and glowing descriptions of hundreds of rose varieties. Half the fun in rose growing lies in choosing your bushes in the first place, but just to make life a bit easier, here are ten of each type that I think are superb. The members of the Royal National Rose Society think so, too, for the varieties are listed in order of preference by these enthusiasts.

Iceberg, the enthusiasts' first choice (see page 27)

Top ten hybrid teas

Silver Jubilee (Introduced in 1978) 75 cm ($2\frac{1}{2}$ ft); a mixture of pinks and creams; moderate scent; glossy green leaves; very good disease resistance.

Grandpa Dickson (1966) 1 m (3 ft); light yellow, very plump and full blooms; moderate scent; glossy deep green leaves; very good disease resistance.

Red Devil (1967) 1.15 m ($3\frac{1}{2}$ ft); bright, light red; very fragrant; deep green glossy leaves; very good disease resistance, but blooms may be rain damaged.

Wendy Cussons (1959) 1 m (3 ft); vibrant cerise pink; heavily scented; glossy deep green leaves; very good disease resistance.

Peace (1942) 1.5 m (5 ft); massive blooms of pale yellow edged with pink; moderate scent; deep green glossy leaves; very good disease resistance.

Fragrant Cloud (1963) 1 m (3 ft); geranium red; very strongly scented; deep green glossy leaves; good disease resistance.

Ernest H. Morse (1965) 1 m (3 ft); rich red; strongly scented; deep green leaves; moderate disease resistance (watch out for mildew).

Pink Favourite (1956) 1 m (3 ft); rich pink; slightly scented; deep glossy green leaves; excellent disease resistance.

National Trust (1970) 75 cm ($2\frac{1}{2}$ ft); crimson red; no scent; deep green leaves; good resistance to disease.

Just Joey (1973) 75 cm ($2\frac{1}{2}$ ft); coppery orange, veined red; slightly scented; deep green leaves; very good disease resistance.

It seems that none of the enthusiasts chose a white hybrid tea. If you want one, the best is undoubtedly:

Pascali (1963) 1 m (3 ft); creamy white; slightly scented; glossy mid-green leaves; good disease resistance.

Top ten floribundas

Iceberg (1958) 1.3 to 1.5 m (4 to 5 ft); pure white; double; some fragrance; glossy green leaves; good disease resistance.

Evelyn Fison (1962) 75 cm (2½ ft); rich, bright red; double; slightly scented; deep green glossy leaves; moderate disease resistance.

Southampton (1972) 1 m (3 ft); coppery orange; double; good scent; deep green glossy leaves; very good disease resistance.

Queen Elizabeth (1954) 2 m (6 ft); light pink; fully double; slightly scented; deep green glossy leaves; very good disease resistance.

City of Leeds (1966) 75 cm (2½ ft); deep salmon pink; double; slightly scented; deep green glossy leaves; moderate disease resistance.

Elizabeth of Glamis (1964) 1 m (3 ft); salmon pink and orange; double; good scent; glossy deep green leaves; poor disease resistance.

Margaret Merril (1977) 1 m (3 ft) white tinged blush pink; fully double; very fragrant; deep green glossy leaves; very good disease resistance.

Matangi (1974) 1 m (3 ft); bright red with white eye; slightly scented; deep green glossy leaves; good disease resistance.

Korresia (1975) 75 cm (2½ ft); bright yellow; fully double; moderate fragrance; glossy green leaves; good disease resistance.

Anne Harkness (1980) 1.45 m (4½ ft); apricot yellow; double; slightly scented; late flowering; matt green leaves; good disease resistance.

Top ten miniatures

Starina (1965) 45 cm ($1\frac{1}{2}$ ft); orange red; fully double; slightly scented.

Darling Flame (1971) 30 cm (1 ft); orange red and yellow; double; no scent.

Baby Masquerade (1956) 30 cm (1 ft); rich pink and yellow; double; no scent.

Pour Toi (1946) 30 cm (1 ft); white tinged yellow; double; slightly scented.

Angela Rippon (1978) 38 cm (15 in); rich salmon pink; double; moderate scent.

Rise 'n Shine (1977) 38 cm (15 in); yellow; fully double; no scent.

Easter Morning (1960) 38 cm (15 in); creamy white; fully double; slightly scented.

Magic Carrousel (1972) 38 cm (15 in); white, edged rich pink; double; slightly scented.

Fire Princess (1969) 45 cm ($1\frac{1}{2}$ ft); bright scarlet; fully double; slightly scented.

Rosina (1951) 30 cm (1 ft); yellow; double; slightly scented.

Plants under roses

The old tradition of leaving bare ground underneath roses is fortunately fizzling out. Apart from being dreary to look at, uncovered soil attracts weeds looking for a home and cats looking for a latrine. Use the space to grow ground-hugging plants that will show off your roses and enjoy their company.

Have a bash at growing alchemilla (lady's mantle), pansies and violas, pulmonaria (lungwort), ajuga (bugle),

Matangi, a floribunda of distinction (see page 27)

aubrieta and arabis, lavender and nepeta (catmint) as edging, stachys (lamb's lugs), lamium (dead nettle), primulas (auriculas and polyanthuses), heuchera (coral bells) and hardy geraniums (cranesbills). Spring bulbs can be planted there, too, and will brighten up the bed or border well in advance of the roses.

Problem pages

There are three problems in particular that it's guaranteed you'll encounter each and every year: greenfly, mildew and black spot. For these it's as well to spray in advance of attack, on the premise that they'll occur if you don't. Other problems can be dealt with as they happen, but don't delay.

Greenfly Spray your bushes with a specific aphicide based on a chemical called pirimicarb. It will kill the greenfly but not ladybirds, lacewings and bees.

Mildew and black spot Both can be deterred in one go by spraying with bupirimate and triforine. Prune out severely mildew-infected stems in winter (they'll be covered with a white powdery deposit), and pick off any black-spotted leaves in summer. Gather up and burn all rose leaves in winter.

Of the other beasts and blights that may rear their ugly thoraxes, these are the commonest:

Leaf-rolling sawfly Causes the leaves to roll under into scrolls. Sometimes grubs are present within the cylinder of leaf. Pick off isolated leaves that are infected. If it's regularly a problem spray in May and again in June with fenitrothion.

Leaf cutter bee Great lumps are cut out of the leaves to give them a scalloped appearance. You'll never catch the bees at it, so this is a problem that has to be tolerated.

Capsid bug Leaves are punctured with brown holes and distorted. Spray with a systemic insecticide as the leaves begin to open in spring.

Caterpillars If the chunks that are eaten out of the leaves are irregular or delineated by the plants' veins, the chances are that caterpillars are eating their fill. Pick off small infestations and throw them on the lawn for the birds. Severe outbreaks can be sprayed with fenitrothion.

Froghoppers The flash name for cuckoo spit. A good squirt with a hosepipe will usually dislodge the insect and the spittle with which it surrounds itself. Fenitrothion is a more lethal cure.

Rust When this disease attacks, rusty brown marks appear on the undersides of the leaves. Spray infected bushes with mancozeb.

Rose black spot

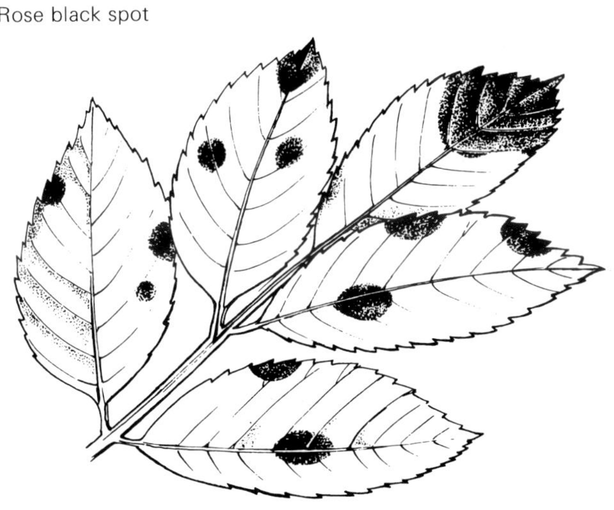

Index

Page numbers in italics refer to illustrations